The King's Butterfly

Story by Gene G. Bradbury
Illustrated by Victoria Wickell-Stewart

BookWilde Children's Books

The King's Butterfly

Copyright ©2015 by Gene G. Bradbury

All rights reserved

All rights reserved. No parts of this book may be reproduced or transmitted in any form or by any means without written permission from the author.

ISBN 978-0-9897585-9-8

Printed in the USA by Createspace Independent Publishing Platform.

Book prepress: Kate Weisel, weiselcreative.com

All inquiries should be addressed to:

BookWilde Children's Books

422 Williamson Rd.

Sequim, WA 98382

www.genegbradbury.com

Author's Dedication

To my lovely wife, Debbie, who believes all life is sacred.

Gene G. Bradbury

Illustrator's Dedication

To Gladys and Fred, my wonderful parents, who chose to adopt me, helping me see things with an artist's eye. All the while fixing scraped knees, taking me on picnics and above all, loving me with all of their hearts.

Victoria Wickell-Stewart

BookWilde Children's Books

Where Is Fergus?

"Fergus, calm down.
This is not about you.
I have written three books about you.
This book is about a butterfly."

"Butterfly, Flutterby!" said Fergus.

"Okay, I will put you on every page if
you promise not to say anything."

"I'll be on every page?"

"Yes, but you must hide.
Children will have to find
you. You will be very
small."

"I can wear no fur," said the King.
"I can wear no feathers," said the Queen.
"Call Wizdrop, the royal Wizard!" shouted the King.

"Wizdrop, your royal Highnesses are allergic to fur and feathers. What should we do for a royal pet?"

"A goldfish, your Highness?"

"How can a goldfish be carried into royal society?" asked the King.

"A butterfly, your Highness?"

"What a delight!" danced the Queen.

"Close the palace windows! The butterfly must be kept inside. Send out a royal decree!" shouted the King.

In the days that followed,
there was a brandishing of butterfly nets.

Orange butterflies alighted on tables.

A butterfly flew through the hallway and rested like a jewel on the King's crown.

If a King could have no fur and a Queen could have no feathers, the butterfly seemed the perfect pet.

But the King's butterfly grew pale. It longed for the milkweed plant outside the window.

The King lowered his head.
"Wise Wizard, send out a royal decree."

**During the Royal Tea
the King raised his scepter
and all the
village windows opened.**

Butterflies flew from cottages.
Butterflies darted from shops.

A cloud of orange wings rose into the sky.

The King's butterfly lifted from the balcony and flew away over the village.

Each year the village awaits the return of the Monarch Butterfly. But none wait more eagerly than the King and Queen.

For a King who can have no fur
and a Queen who can have no feathers,
the Monarch makes the perfect pet.

BookWilde Children's Books

Other Books by the Author

THE MOUSE WITH WHEELS IN HIS HEAD
Meet Fergus who wants to be the first mouse to ride the new Ferris Wheel at the World's Fair. Can a tiny mouse find a way to hitch a ride without being discovered? Follow Fergus's adventure at the 1893 Chicago Exhibition.

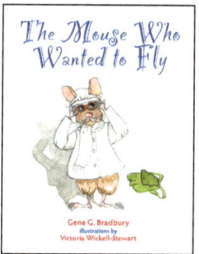

THE MOUSE WHO WANTED TO FLY
Adventure is in Fergus's blood. His success in riding the Ferris Wheel is in the past. When Fergus learns that two brothers, Orville and Wilbur, are going to fly the first powered airplane, Fergus is eager for a new adventure. Is it possible that a mouse can be on the first flight at Kitty Hawk?

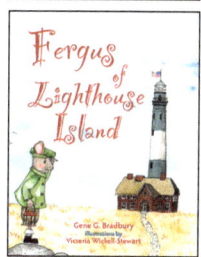

FERGUS OF LIGHTHOUSE ISLAND
Fergus, unlike his great uncle, isn't brave at all. He isn't looking for adventure. But when a hurricane threatens Lighthouse Island, adventure finds him. What will Fergus decide when the hurricane threatens the residents of Mouse Village? It's no place for a mouse who is afraid.

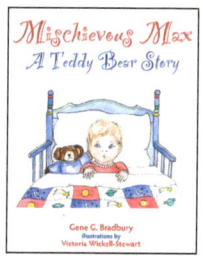

MISCHIEVOUS MAX, A TEDDY BEAR STORY
In Leon's room you will find many teddy bears. Most of them are soft and wonderful to take to bed. But there is one bear who Leon never takes to bed. His name is Max Bear and his fur tickles and his eyes are beastly. Leon knows something else about Max Bear. What if Leon tries sleeping with Max Bear for just one night? Would that be so bad? Leon is about to find out.

THE STAR TREE
"Do the forest animals know about Christmas?" asks Jody. With her grandfather, Jody goes into the forest to the place where the animals gather on Christmas Eve. Jody discovers that the world is a beautiful place to live. The Star Tree invites children to look for Christmas in the natural world.

The above books are illustrated by Victoria Wickell-Stewart
and are available through the author's website: genegbradbury.com;
and through Amazon.com and other retail outlets.

CLOUD CLIMBER
What were his parents thinking, leaving him for three boring weeks at his grandparent's farm? There would be no internet or cable television and what was worse, only Cousin Emily for company. But on a trip to town with his grandfather, Seth learns of Three Friends Hill and the Banshee's Cave. Are these linked to the discovery of a giant kite Seth and Emily find in the old barn? The three weeks literally fly past and the cousins find that Boring Farm is not so boring after all.

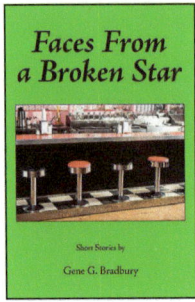

FACES FROM A BROKEN STAR, Short Stories

There was a time when traveling across country one might pull into any small town in America and find a mom and pop cafe. It was a good place to order a fried chicken dinner. Farmers gathered there to compare crop prices and check the weather before working in the field. The local café has disappeared. In these stories you're invited to meet the regulars at the Broken Star Cafe. Some of the characters may sound familiar. Others who will make you laugh and cry.

Poetry Books by Gene G. Bradbury

TRAVELING IN COMPANY

We never travel on our journey alone, but are linked by birth to others. They have walked before us and we follow in their footsteps. Those we come to know best on our travels we call family. From them we learn how to live. Others we meet along the way may lead us to quiet paths of reflection and spiritual practice. In this book of poems the author invites us to look at the many ways we are influenced by others as we travel together.

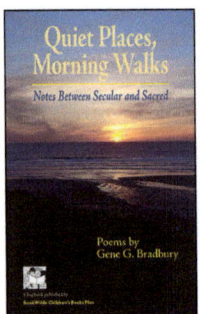

QUIET PLACES, MORNING WALKS:

Notes Between Secular and Sacred

In this book of poetry the author invites the reader to find time each day for quiet and reflection. Each poem is a poetic response to a Psalm verse. The Psalm itself is rewritten in haiku. The book of poetry is prefaced with *morning litanies* to begin the day. The book ends with *evening songs* to end the day. The collection of verse can be used in the morning or evening as a time of quiet and devotion.

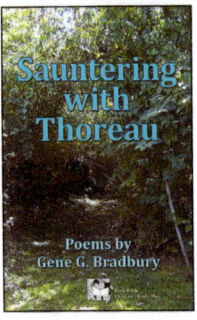

SAUNTERING WITH THOREAU

These poems begin with the author's love of Henry David Thoreau's Journals. Each poem is a reflection on a single quote by Thoreau. The poetry is a brief walk with the nineteenth century naturalist through the woods and along the rivers of Concord. Each poem invites the reader to look intently at the things around them and appreciate the place where they live. In Thoreau's words we are invited to find the kernel of life and not just the husk.

LET ME BE YOUR SERVANT, 100 REFLECTIVE MOMENTS

is both memoir and devotional reading. The book contains 100 short readings from long years of service in parish ministry, hospital chaplaincy, police chaplaincy, prison chaplaincy, and college chaplaincy. Each page reveals the author's choice of reading and thoughts about what it means to live in family and community.

All Gene G. Bradbury books are available through the author's website:
genegbradbury.com;
and through Amazon.com, and other retail outlets.

www.ingramcontent.com/pod-product-compliance
Lightning Source LLC
Chambersburg PA
CBHW042130040426
42450CB00003B/142